# Picture This, Too!

## Picture and Word Sorting for Short and Long Vowels

### by Shari Nielsen-Dunn, M.Ed.

**Teaching Resource Center**

P. O. Box 82777, San Diego, CA 92138-2777
1-800-833-3389
www.trcabc.com

To the people who taught me the most,
going with me from first to sixth grade:
Ana, BreAnna, Chelsey, James, Rachelle, Robert, and Valerri.

Thanks,
Shari

Published by
**Teaching Resource Center**
P.O. Box 82777
San Diego, CA 92138

Illustrations by Linda Starr

©2003 by Teaching Resource Center
All Rights Reserved.
Permission is granted to individual classroom teachers to
reproduce portions of this book for classroom use only.

Printed in the United States of America

# Contents

**Introduction** ................................................... 3

### Section I: Comparing Short to Short Vowel Sounds/Introducing Short Vowel Patterns/Beginning Level Spellers

| | | |
|---|---|---|
| #1 | comparing short a/short o | 19 |
| #2 | comparing short a/short i | 21 |
| #3 | comparing short a/short u | 23 |
| #4 | comparing short i/short a | 25 |
| #5 | comparing short i/short o | 27 |
| #6 | comparing short i/short u | 29 |
| #7 | comparing short o/short a | 31 |
| #8 | comparing short o/short e | 33 |
| #9 | comparing short o/short i | 35 |
| #10 | comparing short o/short u | 37 |
| #11 | comparing short e/short o | 39 |
| #12 | comparing short e/short u | 41 |
| #13 | comparing short u/short a | 43 |
| #14 | comparing short u/short o | 45 |
| #15 | comparing short u/short i | 47 |
| #16 | comparing short u/short e | 49 |

### Section II: Comparing Short to Long Vowel Sounds/Introducing Long Vowel Patterns/Transitional Level Spellers

| | | |
|---|---|---|
| #17 | comparing short a/long a | 52 |
| #18 | comparing short a/long a | 54 |
| #19 | comparing short a/long a | 56 |
| #20 | comparing short o/long o | 58 |
| #21 | comparing short o/long o | 60 |
| #22 | comparing short o/long o | 62 |
| #23 | comparing short i/long i | 64 |
| #24 | comparing short i/long i | 66 |
| #25 | comparing short i/long i | 68 |
| #26 | comparing short e/long e | 70 |
| #27 | comparing short e/long e | 72 |
| #28 | comparing short u/long u | 74 |

### Section III: Comparing Long to Long Vowel Sounds/Introducing Long Vowel Patterns/Transitional Level Spellers

| | | |
|---|---|---|
| #29 | comparing long a/long o | 77 |
| #30 | comparing long a/long o | 79 |
| #31 | comparing long a/long o | 81 |
| #32 | comparing long a/long i | 83 |
| #33 | comparing long i/long o | 85 |
| #34 | comparing long a/long i/long o | 87 |
| #35 | comparing long a/long e | 89 |
| #36 | comparing long a/long e | 91 |

| | | |
|---|---|---|
| #37 | comparing long a/long e | 93 |
| #38 | comparing long e/long o | 95 |
| #39 | comparing long e/long o | 97 |
| #40 | comparing long e/long o | 99 |
| #41 | comparing long a/long u | 101 |
| #42 | comparing long o/long u | 103 |
| #43 | comparing long a/long o/long u | 105 |
| #44 | comparing long i/long u | 107 |
| #45 | comparing long a/long i/long u | 109 |
| #46 | comparing long a/long u | 111 |
| #47 | comparing long o/long u | 113 |
| #48 | comparing long a/long o/long u | 115 |
| #49 | comparing long e/long u | 117 |
| #50 | comparing long a/long e/long u | 119 |
| #51 | comparing long a/long e/long o | 121 |

## Appendix

References and Resources ....................................................123
Index of pictures ............................................................124

# Introduction

Picture and word sorting are an effective ways to teach phonics and develop phonological awareness. As a primary and intermediate classroom teacher, I refined a sequence of picture and word sorting activities to help my students correctly identify and use the sounds and word patterns in our language.

This year, my 6 year old daughter began first grade. What an exciting time for the two of us (probably more so for me than her!). In going over the assessment information with her classroom teacher at the beginning of the year, I noticed that the students in Kiera's reading group were all "using and confusing" the same spelling features in their writing. They would write their short vowel CVC words with extra vowels, and their single-syllable long vowel words with all combinations of letters and no consistency for any one pattern. The group's teacher expressed frustration in knowing what exactly to do to help them cement their learning about spelling patterns in words. She was addressing word work with whole-class shared readings, interactive writing, and basic word work, but she wasn't noticing these concepts transferring into their writing. I suggested we try some sorting activities, and she agreed. We were off to a great, effective collaboration.

We chose sorting over the traditional spelling series for many reasons. First, the spelling series our school had available to us was not well designed. The students were introduced several spelling patterns at the same time and had very little exposure to these. There was little or no opportunity to work with one pattern for an extended period of time. We felt that the students needed to work with both short vowel and long vowel patterns in a sequential, logical manner. Second, since this was a first grade classroom, the development of the children needed to be taken into account. These students were still feeling the sounds in their mouth in addition to hearing the sounds and seeing the pattern. We needed to provide multiple opportunities for the students to really focus on the vowel sounds and word patterns they were encountering. Third, the time available in the classroom for direct instruction in word sounds and patterns in a small group setting was short. The spelling series took up most of that time explaining the directions for the worksheets rather than spending the time focusing on grasping the concepts on the page. We felt that the short time we had could be more effectively spent on grasping the concepts of word sounds and patterns if the routines and procedures were consistent for the activities we would incorporate. Finally, the group of students consisted of 4 students from a variety of home environments. There were boys and girls, an English Language Learner, a student from a low-income background, and two teacher's children—a very diverse little group! We needed to accommodate all our learners in such a way to provide them with avenues of success.

Years back, my school, located near the University of Nevada, Reno, was chosen as a demonstration campus for professors Dr. Donald Bear and Dr. Shane Templeton's developing theories on word study. Dr. Donald Bear utilized my classroom for implementing beginning reading and word study practices. This experience, along with the professors' invaluable book *Words Their Way: Word Study for Phonics, Vocabulary, and Spelling Instruction,* written in collaboration with Marcia Invernizzi and Francine Johnston, exposed me to a whole new way of teaching that involved active exploration and examination of word features that are within a child's stage of literacy development as assessed by the teacher. The book provided me with the rationales, goals, and lists of materials for implementing picture and word sorting in my classroom. Using Words Their Way for the informal assessment information and scope and sequence, and Picture This!: Picture Sorting for Alphabetics, Phonemes, and Phonics, for the pictures and vowel sequence, we began.

## Trying it on

Picture and word sorting dramatically changed my teaching. I came to understand that there's a continuum of learning in language skills and that effectively identifying my students' place on that continuum was the first step. When we moved from picture sorting, connecting it with word patterns, and eventually to word pattern study, my students moved further and faster through the stages of spelling development that they could have without it. This game-like, interactive phonics and spelling activity made sense not only to me, but to them.

Sorting pictures gave the students a stronger oral language foundation than looking at the letter sounds in isolation on a worksheet. They were now dealing with words at a visual level first, so they could analyze the speech sounds that went with the pictures before moving to the printed word. Therefore, they had a phonological underpinning they hadn't had when just looking at written words and letter combinations. They were able to approach phonics at a more concrete level of learning first, then move to the more abstract printed word.

The small group of students in my daughter's class began employing higher-level critical thinking skills to make their decisions while sorting both pictures and, later, words. They were determining the similarities and differences among the pictures and features of words. In addition, I now had the ability to provide multiple examples that the students could work with, discuss, and study. They were able to connect new information to what they already knew. They were able to provide a risk-taking environment for themselves by removing any pictures or words they were unsure of, allowing for success. I was able to use careful observation to decide whether to reuse a sort for reteaching or move on to another sort for new skills. The best part for me was not having to spend time repeating instructions on how to do a new workbook page. The procedure was always the same for picture and word sorting; only the pictures or words would change. The students were enjoying their learning experiences, and I was acquiring valuable assessment information by observing and listening to their discussions about words. Success!

As a literacy coordinator, I have had the opportunity to work with students at many levels. I wondered if picture sorting, moving to word study, would work with older students who were also using but confusing their short and long vowel sounds. I tried it with a small group of students in my own upper grade classroom. First, I found that older students could use the pictures to help them learn, or relearn, the differences between short and long vowel sounds. Once we'd worked with the pictures, listening to the sounds, feeling for the sounds, and discussing the differences between the short and long vowels, we connected the word patterns to those sounds. Having learned to hear and feel the difference in these sounds, the students began to pay attention to the differences in their own writing of words like plan and plain, and hoping and hopping. After cementing this knowledge with pictures and single syllable words, we were able to move on to multi-syllable word study.

Both the students in my daughter's first grade class and the at-risk and Second Language Learners in my upper grade classroom benefited from using the picture and word sorts in this book. Are these sorts really appropriate for upper grade students? Yes! Late Beginning and Early Transitional spellers are of all ages. Older students and Second Language Learners that come to us with various reading, writing, and spelling skills are among the many students who need to work with learning the relationship between letters, sounds, and word patterns. We need to help them understand how words are related to each other in the way they sound, look, and mean so that we could help the students go beyond simplistic, rote knowledge of words to become discoverers of interesting connections between words (Fountas, et. al.).

Now that we know that picture and word sorting works with all types of students, how do we know where to begin with our own classroom? Let's start with looking at the children in the classroom. Take a look at what the students are doing in their spelling and writing. See if there are children who are writing the same type of word features correctly (short vowels—*can, cayn*) and who are using but confusing similar word features (long vowels—*tran, traen*). This would be the group of students that might benefit from working with, discussing, and studying the types of sorts in this book.

# What do they know?

Educational research categorizes children's learning into stages to help with planning instruction for teachers. Students progress through a continuum of literacy learning, acquiring knowledge about spelling and writing from a variety of sources. The picture sorts in *Picture This!* are particularly appropriate for students in the Emergent, Beginning and Early Transitional stages of spelling development. The pictures and word patterns contained in *Picture This Too!* are excellent instructional tools especially for students in the Beginning and Transitional stages of spelling development. This book provides the bridge from pictures to words.

To help identify where students are along the continuum, several informal assessments are available. *Developing Literacy: An Integrated Approach to Assessment and Instruction* (Bear & Barone, 1998) explains several valuable assessments that can be administered in whole-class and small-group settings as well as with individual students. These informal assessments help classroom teachers understand what students know (their independent level), what they're using and confusing (their instructional level), and what's absent in their writing and spelling (their frustration level). Below is a brief overview of the stages for planning:

Children who are **Emergent Readers/Emergent Spellers** may scribble letters and numbers, pretend to read or write, and memorize simple books with high picture support. They are usually able to memorize simple songs and poems. At this stage, some students can recognize some letter sounds, though not necessarily in relation to any word knowledge.

Children who are **Beginning Readers/Letter Name Spellers** often can represent their beginning and ending wounds in their writing and may add incorrect vowels to words. They may read word-by-word in books at their developmental level and may finger-point as they read out loud.

Children who are *Transitional Readers/Within Word Pattern Spellers* may spell most single-syllable short vowel words correctly. They attempt to use silent long vowel markers (t-r-a-n-e for train), and are able to read silently with more fluency and expression. (Bear et. al., 2000).

Careful observation of student work is the key to good instruction. In my early years as a teacher, I always looked at what the kids were missing in their writing and spelling to determine what I should be teaching. That is not the most effective way to design instruction. Now, I look at what the students know to determine their independent level, what they're trying on, or "using but confusing" (Invernizzi, 1992) to determine their instructional level, and what's absent from their spelling to determine their frustration level. I always try to work at the children's instructional level, providing them with the challenge to learn, and the opportunity for success without frustration.

## Where does the group begin?

The basic goal of all picture and word sorting tasks is to compare and contrast word elements, separating or categorizing the examples that go together from those that don't (Bear, et. al. 2000). Begin by modeling a picture sort to a small group of students who share a similar word study need. The children say the names of the pictures and place them into groups under your direction. After doing this with your guidance a few times, students have learned the routines and procedures of picture and word sorting, and can then independently sort similar sets of pictures and words into categories.

After having several discussions with teachers about picture and word sorting, I felt that including a sample lesson of how I've introduced a concept to a small group of students would be helpful. The following sample lesson was used with my daughter's group of Early Transitional Readers and Early Within Word Pattern Spellers. My goal was to help them cement the concepts of short and long vowel sounds, and some of the common spelling patterns.

## Sample Lesson:
## Introducing Long vowel sounds and patterns

One of the most common questions that I'm asked when discussing picture sorting is how to effectively introduce word patterns to young children who are early transitional spellers. The comments usually reflect the fact that introducing and reviewing the short vowels goes well, with the students acquiring the symbol/sound relationship fairly easily. So, then, how do you help students listen and feel for the long vowel sounds so they represent them more accurately in their writing?

Once students become aware that the vowels have different sounds in their reading, they begin to play with their spellings in writing. My daughter was exactly at this place this year. She would spell words like train several different ways: *tran, trane, traen*. More often than not, she'd use the CVC pattern to represent the word, but read it as if it were a long vowel sound. I felt she needed some direct instruction in listening and feeling for long vowel sounds. She was accurate in her representations of all of the short vowel sounds (except confusing the *short e* and *short i* occasionally), so we'd begin there.

Here is the teaching sequence I've developed. In the past few years, I've modified the sequence, and feel that it allows children to work through each sound they encounter in depth. This in-depth exploration coupled with rich discussion allows children to "own" their learning, and incorporate it into their everyday reading and writing experiences. This is the sequence I used this year in working with the small group of students in my daughter's first grade class. I've also included many of the management tips that I've found work well in both picture sorting and word sorting. The days are not necessarily in succession. Most of the time I'm able to do word sorting in a small group setting about two times a week, and alternate with guided reading groupings.

In preparing to work with the small group of students in my daughter's first grade class, I administered the *Developmental Spelling Inventory* from *Words Their Way* (Bear, et al.) to the group. Then, I asked the classroom teacher for some current writing samples. Looking at both of these confirmed that all the students in the small group of four were "using but confusing" (Invernizzi) the long vowel markers in their writing. I listened to the group read several times. All students were able to read several long vowel patterns, but were hesitant to identify them as a long or short vowel sound. Using this assessment information, we began our journey into long vowel land.

I tend to begin with the a sound. The *long a* has a nice group of representative samples of different patterns that tend to be fairly easily generalized to other vowels. So, if the students learn some of the more common patterns for long a, they can generalize to other vowels. In fact, once they begin "owning" the idea of long vowel patterns, they notice them in their reading and ask questions. Perfect teaching opportunity!

# Day 1

Begin the discussion of long and short vowel sounds by introducing a picture sort at the small group table. **Sort #105,** *short a (CVC)/long a (CVCe),* from *Picture This!* is a great place to begin. This sort has two pages, allowing for direct instruction, guided exploration, and independent practice.

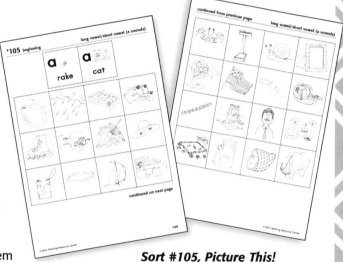

*Sort #105, Picture This!*

1. Have students cut pictures from the **first page** at the small group table. I like to challenge my students to improve the time it takes to cut the pictures and words apart. I have them all get ready for cutting by holding the first page of their picture sort in the open blades of the scissors (which I keep at my table for group work). Then, I watch my clock, saying, "Wait, wait, wait, okay go!" The cutting doesn't need to be perfect; faster is better. I time them, and we work to get it down to one minute for cutting, and 30 seconds for throwing away the scraps and getting ready for sorting.

2. Hand out the "sorting mats" (pieces of 9" x 12" construction paper) to the students for placement of the cut pictures. Each student then begins reading through the pictures out loud, all at the same time. If the student doesn't know a picture, or is unsure of a picture

(isn't sure what to call it, or knows more than one thing it could be called and can't decide on one name) he should set the picture aside. It is too difficult for students to remember a new name to a picture, think about the concepts surrounding that picture, and try to determine where it should go in their sort all at the same time. Allowing students to set the picture aside gives them freedom to do the sort with what they know. Many students add the pictures they've set aside as the other group members share their sorts. Some students don't add them back in. Either is fine, depending on the needs and abilities of the student.

3. Using the same picture cards from the first page of Sort #105 *(Picture This!)*, have the students create a concept sort. You may either direct the students to do an **open sort** (one in which the student chooses the category headings) or a **closed sort** (one in which the teacher chooses the category headings). With younger students, I tend to have them do a closed sort, asking them to do a sort with two columns, such as *alive* and *not alive*. At this time, remind them of the sorting procedures: create a sort, check your sort for changes, and share your sort. Ask for a volunteer to share her sort. Have her read one column of her sort. That student then asks the group if they have any questions or comments. In this way, she becomes the teacher, and must defend or justify her sort. (This also develops students' oral presentation skills.) Remember as the facilitator of the group, you also have the opportunity to ask pointed questions to clarify student thinking. Focus your questioning on directing the student's attention to correct sorting classifications, rather than always showing what the student has done wrong.

4. Again using the picture cards from the first page of Sort #105, ask the students to find the key cards **rake** and **cat** and place them at the top of their sorting mats. Tell them to read each of the other picture cards out loud, *listening and feeling* in their mouth for the sound inside each word. Show them how to compare and contrast each picture card with each key card. For example, if the picture card he picked up was *hat*, the student would compare the sounds like this: *hat, rake/hat, cat.* I think it goes under *cat.* Then, let the students begin sorting and reading each picture out loud. As the facilitator, you're listening to the children, assessing their speed and confidence in their sorting, and helping out as necessary. After the group has sorted and checked their sorts for any changes, ask for a volunteer to share. Have him share **one** column of his sort. Before he begins sharing his sort, have him ask the whole group to "get their pointer fingers ready" so they can see if their sort is like his. He reads down the column using a clear "teacher voice" so that the other students can point at each picture and check their sorts. After sharing the sort, he asks the group if they have any questions or comments. Ask for another student to read the other column, and have her follow the procedure above. It's important that both columns in this sound sort are read, since this is your main focus for the lesson. Discuss how the *short a* and *long a* vowels sound and feel when the students say the words.

8

5. Have the students gather up their cards and hand out the second, uncut page of pictures. This will be their seatwork for the day. They will need to recreate Sort #105, **short a (CVC)/long a (CVCe),** they had made at the small group table, and add the additional pictures to the sort. They will then glue these pictures onto a blank sheet of paper. [I have students glue them on a piece of three-hole punched binder paper, and put the paper in their word study binders (see page 16).] Don't be concerned that there are too many pictures for one piece of paper; students are creative, sometimes gluing pictures on the back or making long tails. They will bring this sort back up to the group table the next day, so it is important that they don't lose it.

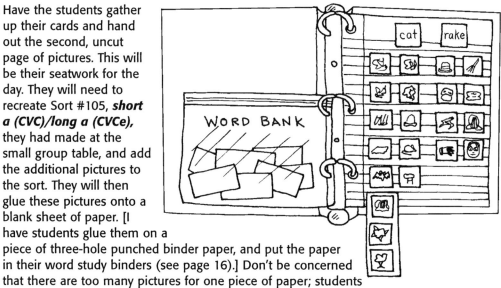

# Day 2

Have the students bring their word study binders to the small group table. Each student can take the sort she had created at her seat from the previous day out of the binder, and then place the binder under her chair. Each student then takes a thin, felt tip marker (color of their choice) from the container placed in the middle of the table. Put a blank piece of chart paper on an easel, and label the chart paper **long a** and **short a** towards the top. Then, ask the group for a *long a* word. A student volunteers a picture, for example sail. The teacher then writes the word on the chart paper under the *long a* column. The students place a checkmark on their picture if they placed it in the *long a* column and a large X over the picture if they placed it in the *short a* column. This continues until a representative sample of words is listed under each column. Remind the students that this is a learning time, and not to worry about the number of X's right now. I feel that the picture sorts students produce can be used as an assessment for the teacher to determine where the group needs to go next. Have the group read down each column on the chart, listening for and feeling for the sounds in each column. If they're early transitional spellers, most of them will get the majority of the pictures in the correct columns. This is considered a "good sort." The students can either turn in their sorts to be sent home to let parents know what they're working on, or they can place them back in their word study notebook to keep as a reminder of their learning.

# Day 3

Now the students are ready to move on to word patterns. However, we need to connect the new learning with what they've already grasped. This is where the pictures and words from *Picture This Too!* work well. Find **Sort #17**, *short a (CVC)/long a (CVCe)* comparison.

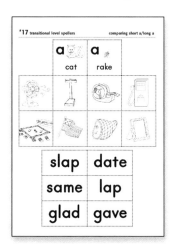

*Sort #17, Picture This Too!*

9

1. Cut the page in half, right below the pictures so that the words and the pictures are separate. Distribute the picture cards to the students in the small group. Follow the procedures listed in Day 1, Step 1 for cutting, reading through the pictures, and setting aside pictures of which the students are unsure. Have the students find the key cards and create a sort *listening and feeling* for the *short a* and *long a* sounds inside the pictures. Ask for a volunteer to share one column. Follow the procedures above for student sharing.

2. Then distribute the word cards from the other half of the sheet. Have the students cut the cards, read the words out loud, and set aside any they're unsure of, following the procedures above. Have the students add these words under the pictures they just sorted, adding to each column. Using a small white board or piece of chart paper on an easel, begin discussing the two patterns represented. Identify the key card *cat* for the *short a* sound. Write the word on the white board. Ask the students which letters are vowels, and which letters are consonants. Write the pattern, CVC under the word so that each label matches up with a letter (phoneme) in the word. Do the same with the long vowel key card *rake*. Write the pattern CVCe under this word. Ask the students for more words to add to the columns. Identify the patterns. Due to time constraints, only a few words will be charted.

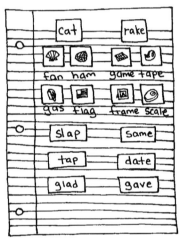

3. The students should carefully gather up their sorts and take them back to their seats to complete as seatwork. They will recreate the sort and glue it on plain binder paper. This time they can try to write the word under the picture (since they've already worked with these pictures in the earlier sort). Once again, the guided practice and direct teaching in the small group setting coupled with the independent practice during the students' seatwork time helps the students have ownership of the concept, and allows for the teacher to assess the learning.

# Day 4

Have students bring up their picture/word sorts to the small group table. Hang the chart that was started on Day 3.

1. Ask a student to volunteer either a *short a* or a *long a* word. At this point, ask the students to only use the word cards. In this way correct (standard) spelling is assured and on the chart. She will say the word and identify the column it should be sorted in. Have her ask the group if they agree or disagree. Each member of the group presents either a thumb up or a thumb down to indicate agreement or disagreement. If the group agrees, she goes to the chart, writes the word in the appropriate column, practicing "teacher writing" (no capitals, correct letter formation, appropriate size), and writes the pattern under the letters. She can then choose the next "teacher" to add to the chart. The process is repeated over and over again. Again, due to time constraints, not all of the words will be charted, but a representative sample will have been. As students become familiar with the procedure, two students can chart at the same time.

2. Before the group's time is over, ask the students what they notice about the columns. (This is the reflective piece of the teaching sequence.) They may state things such as "all of the *short a* words are a CVC pattern" or "all of the *long a* words have a CVCe pattern."

These are the justifications for the sort, and should be recorded at the bottom of each column. Any and all other logical reasons can be recorded. (If a student can logically justify a sort it is considered a "good sort.") This chart can then be posted in the room for future reference. The students can either add their individual picture/word sorts to their word study binder or turn them in to the teacher.

3. Copy the second page of the Sort #17 word sort cards on heavy paper (either construction paper or card stock), and distribute these to the students for seatwork. Remind them of the sorting procedures: read through the cards, set aside any you're unsure of, sort, check your sort for changes, and share your sort. At their seats, they will cut these cards apart, initial the back of each card, and sort these at their seats into the *short a/long a* word columns. These heavy paper word sort cards will not be glued down on paper, but rather will be stored for future use in word banks. If time permits, have them write the word sort down on a piece of paper, or if time is short, have them share their sort with a buddy, and then rubber band the sort and put it in their word bank baggie. (See *Words Their Way* for more information on word banks.)

# Day 5

Have students bring either their written sorts or their word banks with this week's rubber banded word cards to the small group table.

1. Have students re-create the sort at the table using the cards from their word banks. Ask for a volunteer to share one of the columns. Follow the sharing procedures from above. Check for accuracy. At this point, all the students should be very accurate in the sorting between *short a (CVC)* and *long a (CVCe)*. Depending on time, the students, as a group, can add to the chart started on Day 4, or, at their seats, write down the sort on paper to add to their word study binders.

2. Now that students understand the routines and procedures of picture and word sorting, they should be able to do some of the initial sorting at their seats. This will allow them to make decisions as to how the pictures and words should be sorted, and will allow the teacher to assess their work and make decisions on where the lesson should go, based on how accurately the students are sorting.

3. This next step can be done at the end of group time on Day 5, so that students will be ready for sorting on Day 6. Distribute the **Sort #18**, *short a (CVC)/long a (CVVC) (Picture This! Too)*. Remind the students of the sorting procedure stated previously. Have them read through the cards at the table, but don't have the students cut them at the table this time. They will cut, sort, and glue the sorts at their seat during seatwork time. Students will put this picture/word sort in their word study binder so that it can be discussed during the next group word study time.

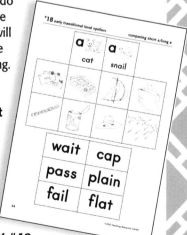

***Sort #18, Picture This Too!***

11

## Day 6

Have the students bring their picture/word Sort #18, *short a (CVC)/long a (CVVC),* to the small group table.

1. Check over the group's work to see that everyone has fairly accurately sorted both the pictures and the words. Early transitional writers should be able to do this fairly accurately and independently.

2. Repeat the steps above for charting and discussion, allowing the students to be the "teachers" as much as possible. Remember to make a point of reflecting throughout the discussion as to what the students notice in each column before excusing the group.

3. At the end of group time, distribute the word cards from Sort #18 copied on heavy paper stock. The students can read through these cards at the table and take them to their seat for seatwork. Remind them that these will not be glued down on paper, but will be cut, the backs initialed, sorted at their desk, and written down on paper during seatwork time. Then put the cards in their word bank with a rubber band around them. They can use the same rubber band that was around the last *CVC/CVCe* sort, leaving these cards loose in their word bank.

## Day 7

Have the students bring their written word sort (Sort #18) to the small group table.

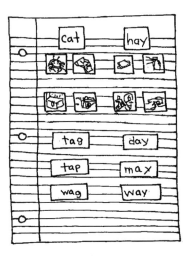

1. Allow the students to complete the charting of the patterns that was started on Day 6. Follow the sharing and charting procedures listed above, letting the students be the "teacher" as much as possible. Ask them what they notice about the two columns, and write their observations down under each column.

2. Bring the *short a (CVC)/long a (CVCe)* chart over and place it next to the *short a (CVC)/long a (CVVC)* chart. Ask the children what they notice. Reflect with the students, discussing their observations.

3. Distribute the next picture/word sort: **Sort #19,** *short a (CVC)/long a (CVV)*. Have the students read through the pictures and words at the small group table. They probably will have some observations before they even begin sorting. Allow the discussion to continue, and then send them off to complete the sort at their seats.

# Day 8

1. At this point, allow the students to chart the new pattern that they've sorted following the sharing and charting procedures above. However, you can add two more columns to the chart so that all four patterns are represented: *CVC, CVCe, CVVC, CVV*. If you think the students are ready, based on the comments they have made during discussion, allow them to look through their word study binder to add to the chart as they see fit. Remember to let the students be the "teachers" as much as possible.

2. Discuss what they are noticing, and chart their generalizations and observations under each column. This chart should be posted somewhere in the room for reference. The other charts can be hung behind this one, since this summarizes the students' learning to this point.

3. Decide, based on the group's accuracy in sorting and discussion in the group, whether to have the group do the *short a (CVC)/long a (CVV)* word sort (copied on heavier paper stock) or go on a word hunt in known text (i.e., a poem that has been shared in class and with which all group members are fairly comfortable) for the four patterns that have been learned. If you decide to have the group do the sort, follow the procedures previously outlined for sorting at the student's seat. However, if you decide to send the students on a word hunt, you will need to model the hunt first. (For more information on word hunting see *Words Their Way*.)

4. Choose a piece of known text and read it with the students, listening and feeling for short and long a words. When a *long a* or a *short a* word is encountered, have the students record the word on a piece of binder paper, under the appropriate column. After some guided practice in the group, students can do this at their seat, using known text from their book boxes, Personal Readers, and writing around the room. All words should be recorded and put in their word study binder. Students will undoubtedly write down words that have an a in them, but that are neither short nor long a. Don't worry, we'll deal with this at the group.

# Day 9

Have the students bring up their word hunts or their word sort. If they have completed the *short a (CVC)/long a (CVV)* word sort, follow the procedures above and complete the chart that was started on Day 8. If they went on a word hunt, they'll want to share the words they've found.

1. You will need to direct the group quite a bit during the charting. Name the chart with **Word Hunt** at the top, then label each column: *short a, long a,* and *odds and ends sound.* Ask for a volunteer to share a word. Ask the students the correct column in which to write the word. If the word is one of the patterns that has been introduced (*CVC, CVCe, CVVC, CVV*) then ask him if he can identify the pattern. If the word is a *short a* or a *long a* pattern that hasn't been introduce, don't ask for him to identify the pattern. The students may want to know what the pattern is, and together, students and teacher, can discover the pattern. Some students will ask, and some will not. Let them be the

guide to what they're ready to learn. Try very hard not to "tell" too much, but to allow them to "tell" you what they're ready to learn by asking questions. Some students will have found words that do not have a long or short a sound. A word they might find would be *was*. Ask them if it sounds like either of the words in the *short a* or the *long a* column (compare and contrast it to the words at the top of each column, asking students to hear and feel the sounds). Ask them where they think this word should be sorted. Write the word in the *odds and ends sound* column. You can point out that you think it's interesting that not all words with an *a* always fit into either the *short a* or the *long a* sound columns. Then, pose a challenge to the students to find other words that don't fit into the two columns. These can be added to the chart at any time. Chart as many words as time allows, and ask for observations and generalizations to be entered at the bottom of each column.

2. You will need to determine if the students need to learn the more complicated and less common long a patterns at this time (typically older students) or to move on to the next long vowel (typically younger students and ESL students). Based on informal observations made at the small group, and on independent work, you can pick and choose from *Picture This Too!* and meet the needs of these early transitional writers. The ultimate goal is to move these students forward into incorporating the patterns they're learning into their everyday writing.

**Group Generated Word Hunt Chart**

# When You Sort

| | |
|---|---|
| cat<br><br><br><br>1. read through the cards | 2. set aside any you're unsure of |
| 3. sort | 4. check your sort for changes |
| 5. share your sort | 6. justify your sort |

# Word Study Materials I Use

**Personal Readers:** Each student in the class has a Personal Reader. These are discussed at length in *Words Their Way*. The personal readers that my students use are 1" binders. These binders contain copies of independent reading material. The passages could be whole class poems, ditties, or rhymes that we've memorized or learned well enough to read on our own. They could also contain our guided reading group leveled book, typed on one page, and illustrated by the student. Each passage in the Personal Reader is dated, and added to the binder. In this way, each student has a Personal Record of independent reading material. These passages can be used for word hunts in order to gather more words to add to a particular sort, providing more exemplars to discuss. Some teachers design a pocket (or insert a three-hole punched folder) for the binder. They have the students keep the current small group reading book in that pocket for easy access. Each time the students move to the small group table for guided reading, they bring their Personal Readers with them.

**Word Study Notebooks:** Each student in the class has a Word Study Notebook. There are many different types of notebooks. Some teachers use the spiral, lined paper notebooks (about 70 sheet size), while other teachers prefer three-ring binders. I choose to use a three ring binder. When a child completes a word or picture sort, either glued down on the three-hole punched paper or written down on three-hole binder paper, they put it in the front of the word study notebook. This reduces the number of sorts that are lost in the classroom. This provides the student with an on-going record of their learning since the sorts will be in somewhat of a chronological order. In the very front of this binder is their word bank. A word bank is a storage place for known words, and words that the students are working on in word study. I use a freezer weight, quart size, Zip-Loc type baggie for the word banks. I insert one side of the baggie in a three-hole punch, only using two of the hole punches, to punch two holes in the side of the baggie. In this way, this bag can be inserted into the binder for safe keeping. This helps eliminate lost word banks. When it is time for word study at the small group table, the students bring their Word Study Notebook with them to the group table. Word Banks and Word Study Notebooks are introduced in *Words Their Way*.

# Types of Sorts

There are many types of sorts that one can use with students in their word investigations. I'll discuss the ones I use the most.

An **Open Sort** is when the students choose the categories. Sometimes, the teachers need to model a few different options to get the creative juices flowing. Children can be much more creative than adults, however, so be prepared. Some examples that a teacher may want to model would be a concept sort (using the meaning of the pictures or words to group them together, rather than the spelling or sound patterns), beginning sound sort, ending sound sort, number of syllables, rhyming words, or parts of speech. Try to stay away from number of letters in a word. Once that has been introduced, it's hard to get the kids to do other sorts.

A **Closed Sort** is when the teacher decides the categories. The teacher usually chooses key cards to represent the concepts to be covered in the lesson. The students then sort the rest of the cards under the key cards in each category. Closed sorts can be concept sorts (i.e., alive/not alive) or sound sorts (i.e., short/long vowel sounds), or pattern sorts (i.e., CVCe, CVVC, CVV). Teachers need to carefully choose the key cards so that there is no confusion as to the intent of the lesson.

For more information on the stages and practical applications for these sorting suggestions, see *Words Their Way*. If you'd like to see students doing all kinds of sorts, there is a *Words Their Way Video* available for purchase.

## What's Really Important to Remember?

When I began learning about word study, my word knowledge grew incredibly. I'm pretty sure that I just "absorbed" the spelling I needed to in order to make it through life. I knew that I didn't know enough about words to be able to teach it to someone else. The English language seemed so confusing, even at the lowest levels. What would I say if a student asked me why a CVC word like *c-a-t* was pronounced with a *short a* sound and another CVC word, *w-a-s,* was pronounced with a *short u* sound? Well, I learned very quickly that I wasn't going to know the answers to those questions, and that it was okay not to know. I would tell the students that that was a very good question, write the word on the bottom of the chart we were working on, put a question mark next to it, and challenge the students to find other words that were similar to it. In this way, I was able to honor the students' question, show that teachers don't know everything, and allow the students to take the lead in generating a generalization for the word. (I also began acquiring some word origin dictionaries and some word history books to add to my classroom collection so I could discover why words were spelled the way they are in our language.) What I'm saying is to jump in and give word study a try. Learn with your students.

One of my favorite sayings is "teachers can teach whatever they want, but students will learn what they're ready to learn." Remember to start with the children. See what they're "using but confusing" and begin there. They're showing you what they're ready to solidify in their learning. Allow them to take the lead. Remember that social interaction and learning from your proximal partner (someone who is close to your developmental level in a certain concept or area) is the best way to incorporate new learning (Vygotsky, 1978). Allow the children to lead the groups, ask the questions, and defend their ideas. You'll be surprised how much YOU learn from their discussions. Always, always have a reflection time built in to your lesson. This is where you'll help the children "see" what your goal was for the lesson. It will also allow you to "see" where the students' understanding of the concept is. This will help you drive instruction for the next lesson.

As a professional, you can make the decision of where to begin word study with your students. Pick and choose from *Picture This!* for picture sorting, *Picture This Too!* for connecting word patterns to earlier picture sorts, and other professional titles for extensive word sorting. Use your professional judgment and careful observation of student work to determine which sorts to use, which to skip, and where to begin. If you're unsure, just remember that a step backward is a step forward. I tend to be more conservative in introducing new material, to see what the students already know before jumping in deeper. Most importantly, don't forget to have fun with sorting. Your students will!

# Section I

## Comparing Short to Short Vowel Sounds Introducing Short Vowel Patterns
### Beginning Level Spellers

Vowels are the musical notes of language. Without the music of the vowels, the consonants are just noise. Your students are ready to begin studying the vowel sounds when they can write words from memory with vowels in them. At this point, they may not always write the correct vowel, but they are beginning to hear them, and represent them in some way in their writing. For instance, a student may spell the word *bet* as *bat*. This student is showing not only a readiness to begin studying short vowel sounds, but also the ability to use his knowledge of letter names (the actual name of each letter) and the feel of the vowel to write words (Bear, et. al., 2003). Students at this level typically do not have a huge amount of words they can read by sight. This is why picture sorting is so valuable. You can still introduce the sounds of the vowels and the corresponding letters without using words. This forces the students to really pay attention to the way the vowels sound and feel before moving on to the words, and word patterns.

I've organized this section in a sequence of study that has worked well with several groups of students. Begin sorting sounds with obvious contrasts first. Stay away from comparing vowels that are close in sound and feeling (*short i/short e,* and *short e/short a*). You may choose to begin with vowel combinations that are not in my sequence, based on the assessments and writing samples from your groups of students. Pick and choose where you think your group is ready to begin, and move on from there. Use the sample lesson listed in the introduction to help with the management tips and sorting steps.

If you're introducing a letter sound for the first time, you'll probably want to begin with a *closed sound* sort (see page 8). A detailed sample lesson is included in the introduction (see page 6). Use the sample lesson to create your own small group interactions.

When sorting, remember that a justified sort is a good sort. In Sort #1, a student may call the picture of the word *hop* a *bunny*. They may want to create an *odds and ends* column, since *bunny* doesn't fit under either the *cat* or *dog* key cards. The student has used logical thinking to create what is considered a "good sort." Allow the student to have an *odds and ends* column as long as it is the shortest column. If it is longer than the other columns, the student may need help understanding some of the pictures, or may need a review of the features being examined.

You'll notice that I didn't focus on the word families (hat, bat, rat) as the primary focus. I focused on the vowel sounds, so students would make the generalization across several word families, rather than only listening for the rhyming words.

You'll also notice that I didn't match word cards to the picture cards. I did this on purpose. In this way, students can use the knowledge they gain from the patterns discovered in sorting the words to attempt to write the names of the pictures on the picture cards. This won't happen in the beginning, but will almost naturally occur as students become more comfortable with sorting, and making logical generalizations about sounds, words, and patterns. The pictures are repetitious, and can help build children's sight word vocabulary over repeated usage if the students begin to write the name of the picture on the card.

When charting the patterns, use what **you** know. When I label (C=consonant, V=vowel) under each letter on chart paper in a small group setting, I try to be consistent and demonstrate a definite pattern to the students. When I come to a word like *stop* in Sort #1, I consider the "st" a blend, and say that the two consonants work together. When two consonants work together and we can hear both sounds, it is considered to be a blend and is one unit: which would have a line drawn under it and a *C* for consonant written under it. If a word has a digraph in it (sh, ph, th, etc.), I tell the children that these two consonants make a new sound, different than either separate sound, and that this too is considered one unit and has a *C* for consonant written under the digraph. In this way, the words in this section should all be CVC pattern words, helping children make the generalization about the short vowel sound across the vowels.

#1 beginning level spellers     comparing short a/short o

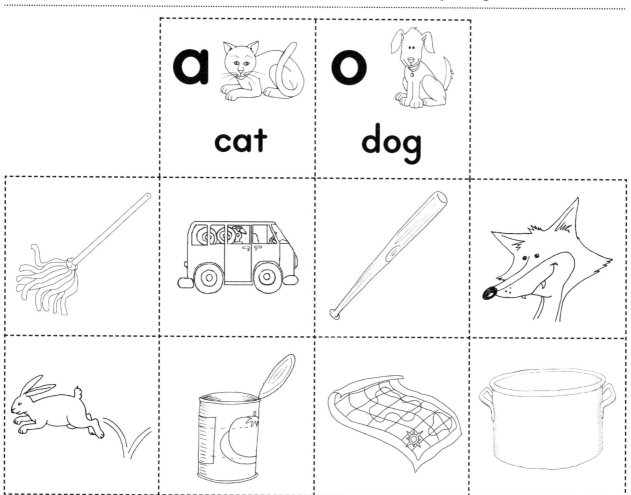

**#1** beginning level spellers		comparing short a/short o

| stop | bag | hot |
| --- | --- | --- |
| box | cob | fan |
| pan | hat | block |
| gas | jam | frog |
| | | |
| | | |
| | | |

# #2 beginning level spellers

comparing short a/short i

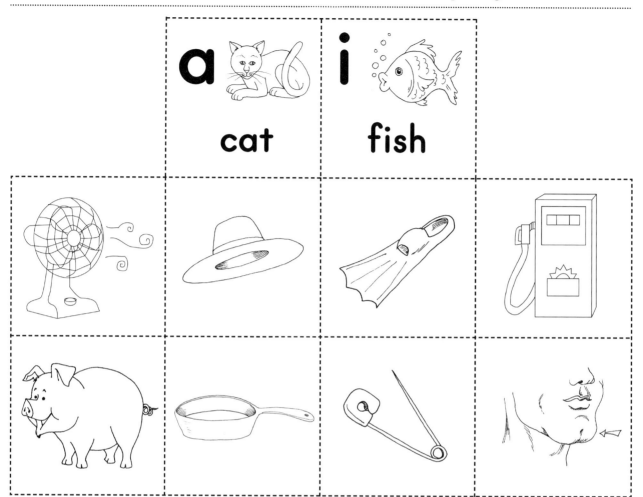

**#2** beginning level spellers  comparing short a/short i

| dish | flag | jam |
|---|---|---|
| crab | sit | man |
| can | kiss | dig |
| skip | chick | bat |
| | | |
| | | |
| | | |

# #3 beginning level spellers
## comparing short a/short u

#3 beginning level spellers  comparing short a/short u

| skunk | truck | grab |
| --- | --- | --- |
| thumb | trap | tan |
| bag | tub | mug |
| nut | bad | sat |

# #4 beginning level spellers
## comparing short i/short a

**#4** beginning level spellers	comparing short i/short a

| lick | rip | sack |
| --- | --- | --- |
| clam | drill | tap |
| than | win | big |
| drag | dad | hit |

# #5 beginning level spellers
## comparing short i/short o

#5 beginning level spellers — comparing short i/short o

| sick | boss | sock |
| --- | --- | --- |
| flip | spill | drop |
| jog | skin | mob |
| rig | lot | lit |

#6 beginning level spellers     comparing short i/short u

**#6 beginning level spellers** — comparing short i/short u

| trick | bun | trip |
| --- | --- | --- |
| hum | will | tug |
| win | nut | club |
| bump | big | fit |

# #7 beginning level spellers

### comparing short o/short a

#7 beginning level spellers          comparing short o/short a

| top | black | rag |
| song | rash | shop |
| frog | band | sob |
| bat | dot | pad |

#8 beginning level spellers — comparing short o/short e

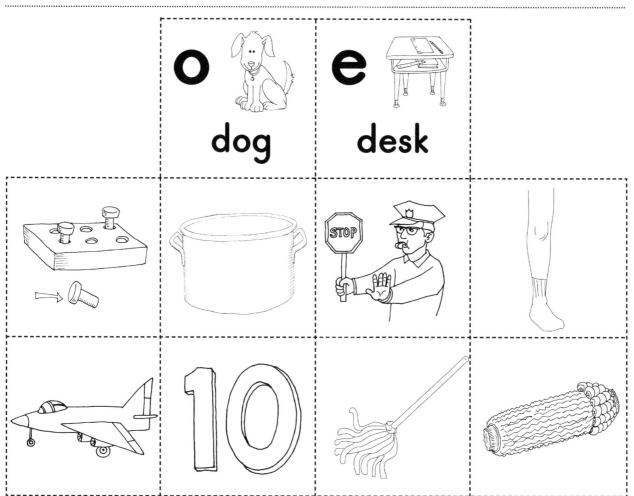

#8 **beginning level spellers**  **comparing short o/short e**

| vet | then | long |
| --- | --- | --- |
| red | loss | wed |
| flock | log | well |
| nest | hop | blob |

# #9 beginning level spellers

## comparing short o/short i

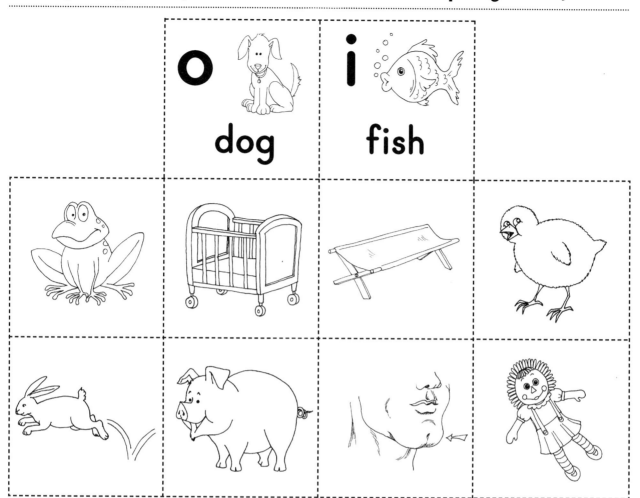

**#9** beginning level spellers — comparing short o/short i

| bob | six | this |
|---|---|---|
| skid | box | trot |
| crop | rid | shock |
| fix | hid | long |

# #10 beginning level spellers

**comparing short o/short u**

**#10** beginning level spellers　　　comparing short o/short u

| jump | bun | dock |
| --- | --- | --- |
| hum | flop | bog |
| blob | dot | dug |
| hub | cup | knot |

# #11 beginning level spellers

**comparing short e/short o**

| e — desk | o — dog |
|---|---|
| web | hem |
| box | log |
| not | gem |

# #11 beginning level spellers
## comparing short e/short o

| dot | nest | snob |
| --- | --- | --- |
| peg | dog | vest |
| pop | tent | bell |
| flock | dress | toss |

# #12 beginning level spellers

comparing short e/short u

#12 beginning level spellers — comparing short e/short u

| best | hut | stub |
| peck | peg | plug |
| drum | cell | then |
| gun | pup | bled |

#13 beginning level spellers       comparing short u/short a

| u — bus | a — cat |

cut | tax
bun | bus
wag | can

**#13** beginning level spellers    comparing short u/short a

| mud | scab | shut |
| --- | --- | --- |
| sand | plus | cash |
| sum | lad | thud |
| that | fan | dust |

# #14 beginning level spellers

comparing short u/short o

bus  dog

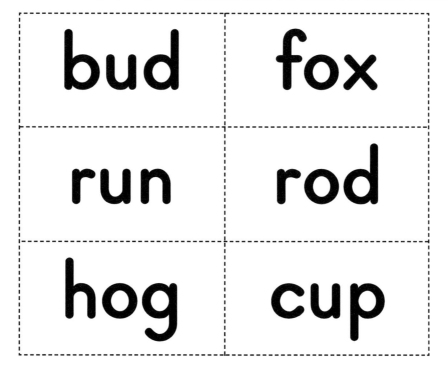

| bud | fox |
| run | rod |
| hog | cup |

©2003 Teaching Resource Center

#14 beginning level spellers — comparing short u/short o

| duck | just | toss |
| --- | --- | --- |
| rust | soft | lost |
| hot | suck | gut |
| lock | pop | tug |

# #15 beginning level spellers

comparing short u/short i

**#15** beginning level spellers		comparing short u/short i

| lump | fuzz | strip |
| --- | --- | --- |
| run | lid | huh |
| jig | mud | twig |
| this | puff | fix |
|  |  |  |
|  |  |  |
|  |  |  |

#16 beginning level spellers — comparing short u/short e

u — bus
e — desk

yes · web
pup · rug
hem · rut

**#16** beginning level spellers — comparing short u/short e

| cuff | pump | help |
| --- | --- | --- |
| best | cluck | less |
| pest | gem | met |
| gun | bum | tug |

# Section II
## Comparing Short to Long Vowel Sounds
## Introducing Long Vowel Patterns
### Early Transitional Level Spellers

Your students are ready to study the differences between long and short vowels when they begin experimenting with the spellings of the many vowel patterns of English. They "use but confuse" these patterns (Invernizzi, Abouzeid, & Gill, 1994). Students may be spelling the word *train* as *t-r-a-n-e*, *t-r-a-i-n-e*, or *t-r-a-e-n*, as they explore how to create the long vowel sound. At this stage, students understand that letter name/sound alone does not indicate spelling.

To begin this study, students should compare what they know with the new information you're introducing. Therefore, I've organized this section in such a way that short and long vowel sounds can be compared and contrasted sequentially, if desired. Once the students have effectively sorted the short and long vowel pictures, noticing the differences in the way the vowels sound and feel, they can begin comparing and contrasting the simple word patterns introduced in this section.

Read over the information in Section I that discusses comparing and contrasting pictures, knowing what a "good sort" is, what a justified sort is, what an *odds and ends* column is, and how to chart the vowel patterns under the CVC pattern words. Then return to this section.

A discussion comparing long and short vowels from Sort # 17 might sound like this: "Let's see which key card the word *date* might go under. Say it with me now: *date, cat/ date, rake*. Remember, we're listening for the sound inside the words. What do you think students? Yes, *date* has the same *long a* sound that we hear in the word *rake*. Let's put *date* in the *long a* column."

When you're ready to chart the patterns of the words, remember that blends (tr, bl, st, etc…) and digraphs (th, sh, ph, etc…) are considered one unit, and have only a C written under them to acknowledge them as consonants. Vowels have a V written under them to signify long and short vowel sounds. And, for the *silent e* at the end of a work, I choose to write a lower case *e* under it, so that it stands out as a feature. However, some teachers choose to write a V under the *silent e* to show it is a vowel. Each teacher will make her own decision based on what's comfortable to her.

Remember, when you introduce long vowel patterns that you make sure you return to the pictures when introducing new vowel sounds. Make sure the students are constantly *listening and feeling* for the different sounds that the vowels are making. This will help them in their writing when they're trying to spell short and long vowel sounds. This is particularly important in working with Second Language Learners. Differentiating between long and short vowel sounds, and trying to get a handle on the spellings of these is very difficult in the English language.

#17 early transitional level spellers — comparing short a/long a

52 ©2003 Teaching Resource Center

# #17 early transitional level spellers — comparing short a/long a

| hat | name | pass |
| --- | --- | --- |
| flat | jack | race |
| cape | plane | ask |
| page | fast | gate |

#18 early transitional level spellers   comparing short a/long a

54  ©2003 Teaching Resource Center

#18 early transitional level spellers — comparing short a/long a

| rain | path | slap |
| --- | --- | --- |
| last | wait | jack |
| sat | pail | nail |
| sail | mail | chain |

#19 early transitional level spellers    comparing short a/long a

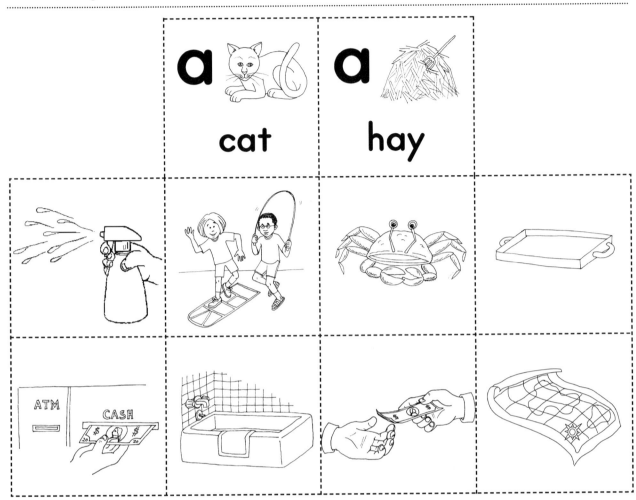

56    ©2003 Teaching Resource Center

#19 early transitional level spellers    comparing short a/long a

| gray | pack | play |
| --- | --- | --- |
| lay | that | pad |
| say | stay | pay |
| tap | nap | had |
|  |  |  |
|  |  |  |
|  |  |  |

# #20 early transitional level spellers

**comparing short o/long o**

58 ©2003 Teaching Resource Center

**#20** early transitional level spellers  comparing short o/long o

| shot | choke | got |
|------|-------|-----|
| rode | fog | hope |
| rob | vote | pop |
| stone | flop | note |

#21 early transitional level spellers         comparing short o/long o

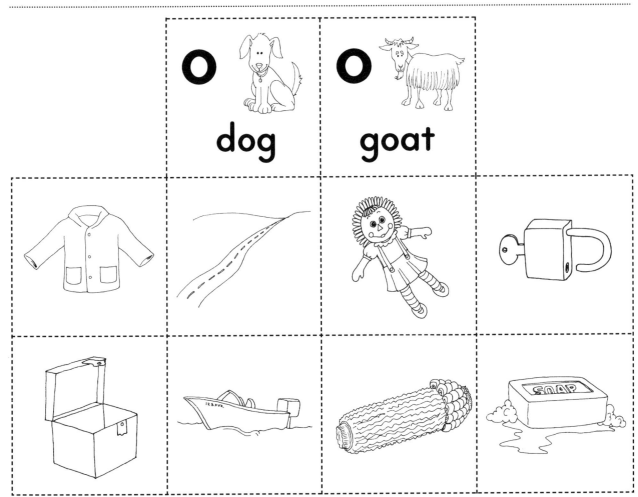

# #21 early transitional level spellers — comparing short o/long o

| soap | soft | moan |
| cost | loaf | frog |
| coach | dog | toad |
| moth | coal | clock |

#**22** early transitional level spellers     comparing short o/long o

# #22 early transitional level spellers
## comparing short o/long o

| throw | tow | blow |
| --- | --- | --- |
| rot | knot | pot |
| frost | shop | drop |
| crow | grow | know |
| | | |
| | | |
| | | |

#23 early transitional level spellers    comparing short i/long i

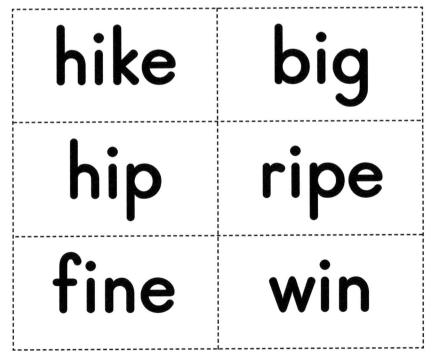

# #23 early transitional level spellers — comparing short i/long i

| | | |
|---|---|---|
| nice | ride | sit |
| life | hit | dig |
| sick | thin | list |
| wife | price | mine |

#24 early transitional level spellers    comparing short i/long i

# #24 early transitional level spellers

## comparing short i/long i

| by | zip | cry |
| rip | dry | lick |
| sly | pick | sky |
| dish | try | clip |

#**25** early transitional level spellers — comparing short i/long i

pit  might
sit  tight
sight  wig

# #25 early transitional level spellers — comparing short i/long i

| miss | quick | chin |
|---|---|---|
| fin | bright | flight |
| bill | light | blight |
| drip | height | slight |

#26 early transitional level spellers                  comparing short e/long e

70                                          ©2003 Teaching Resource Center

# #26 early transitional level spellers — comparing short e/long e

| pen | wheel | sled |
| --- | --- | --- |
| green | hen | fell |
| speed | keep | step |
| neck | cheese | weed |
|  |  |  |
|  |  |  |
|  |  |  |

#**27** early transitional level spellers … comparing short e/long e

# #27 early transitional level spellers — comparing short e/long e

| vet | peach | meat |
| --- | --- | --- |
| beat | then | red |
| shell | teach | peg |
| seat | real | deck |

#**28** early transitional level spellers    comparing short u/long u

# #28 early transitional level spellers — comparing short u/long u

| cute | tune | duck |
| --- | --- | --- |
| spun | huge | gum |
| rude | fume | mug |
| club | cut | prune |

# Section III
## Comparing Long to Long Vowel Sounds
## Introducing Long Vowel Patterns
### Transitional Level Spellers

Your students are ready to examine the complex patterns of long vowel words when they are consistently marking their long vowel patterns in their writing. They may not be spelling their single-syllable long vowel words correctly, but they differentiate between short and long vowel words. For example, they consistently spell the word *tap* (what you might do on a drum with a drumstick) as *t-a-p*, where they spell the word *tape* (what you'd use to stick two items together with) as *t-a-i-p, t-a-e-p,* or some other combination of letters. They are acknowledging that they can hear and feel the difference between short and long vowel sounds, and that they're ready to study the patterns that make these sounds. Again, they are "using but confusing" their knowledge of long vowel patterns.

Students should compare what they know with the new information you're introducing. I've organized this section to move on from where the students left off in Section II. Students are going to compare and contrast various patterns that were introduced in Section II, extending their understanding of long vowel patterns across the vowels.

A discussion of Sort #29, comparing *long a* and *long o* CVCe patterns might sound like this: "Let's see which column the word vase might go under. Say it with me now: *vase, rake/vase, rope.* Remember, we're listening and feeling for the vowel sound in the middle of the word. What do you think students? Yes, *vase* goes under the key card *rake*. They both have the same *long a* sound, and *long a* pattern." When charting the words, remember to include all blends and digraphs as a single unit, writing a C underneath the unit. In this way, you're students will be able to make generalizations about the long vowel patterns they encounter in this section.

In this section, some of the words on the word cards **do** match the picture cards. Because of a limited number of words within a particular pattern (Sort # 48, the word card *suit*, and the picture card *suit*), some had to match. Students will notice this I'm sure. Just use your good teacher skills, and congratulate them on paying close attention.

Single-syllable long vowel words have some interesting features that you'll need to explain to the students. The letter *y* can be both a consonant and a vowel. I tell the students that when it sounds like a consonant (as in the word *yellow*) then it is usually a consonant. If it sounds like a vowel (as in the word *hay*) then it is usually considered to be a vowel. Therefore, the pattern for *hay* is CVV. The letter *w* can also work in much the same way. When it sounds like a consonant (as in the word *went*) it is usually a consonant. When it sounds like a vowel (as in the word *tow*) then it is usually considered a vowel. Therefore, the pattern for tow is CVV. As word study continues, students will find examples and non-examples (for instance, *shower*) for these observations. This is why it is important to stay away from the word "rule" and move toward the word "generalization" instead. Generally, the concepts stated above occur.

Use your classroom observation and informal assessments to drive your instruction particularly in this section. Students will be able to quickly generalize some word patterns, and need more time and interaction with other word patterns. Pick and choose what fits with your word study groups.

# #29 transitional level spellers

comparing long a/long o

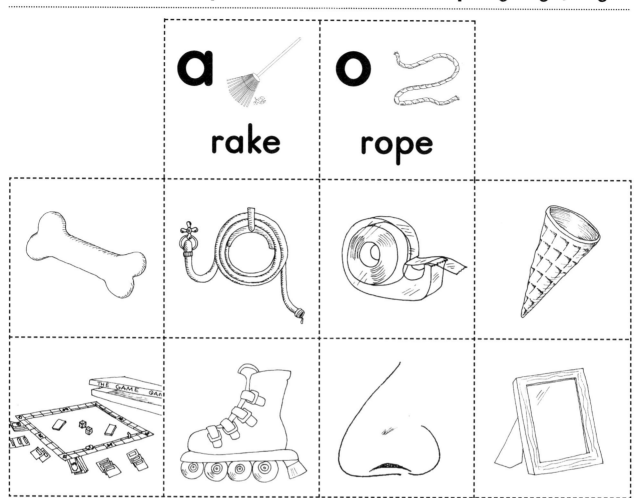

| robe | vase |
| lane | zone |
| woke | lace |

**#29** transitional level spellers  comparing long a/long o

| grape | mate | whole |
|---|---|---|
| spoke | scale | tame |
| gate | throne | mole |
| late | close | drove |

#30 transitional level spellers — comparing long a/long o

**#30** transitional level spellers  comparing long a/long o

| goal | loan | great |
| --- | --- | --- |
| float | wait | foam |
| break | waist | coal |
| moat | rain | pain |
| | | |
| | | |
| | | |

#31 transitional level spellers · comparing long a/long o

| say | show |
| low | day |
| tow | may |

**#31** transitional level spellers  comparing long a/long o

| gray | grow | play |
| --- | --- | --- |
| clay | know | slay |
| show | stay | way |
| blow | crow | flow |
|  |  |  |
|  |  |  |
|  |  |  |

# #32 transitional level spellers

comparing long i/long a

**#32** transitional level spellers    comparing long i/long a

| vase | jade | tide |
|------|------|------|
| slice | tale | ripe |
| slave | tame | wipe |
| file | whale | spice |

#33 transitional level spellers         comparing long i/long o

# #33 transitional level spellers — comparing long i/long o

| stove | woke | smile |
| --- | --- | --- |
| froze | mice | size |
| dome | phone | hike |
| ripe | slice | smoke |

#34 transitional level spellers        comparing long a/long i/long o

| a rake | i bike | o rope |

tape | tide
lake | vote
life | hope

| whole | slope | pole |
| --- | --- | --- |
| throne | stripe | hike |
| whale | wipe | date |
| lime | take | save |
| | | |
| | | |

#35 transitional level spellers — comparing long e/long a

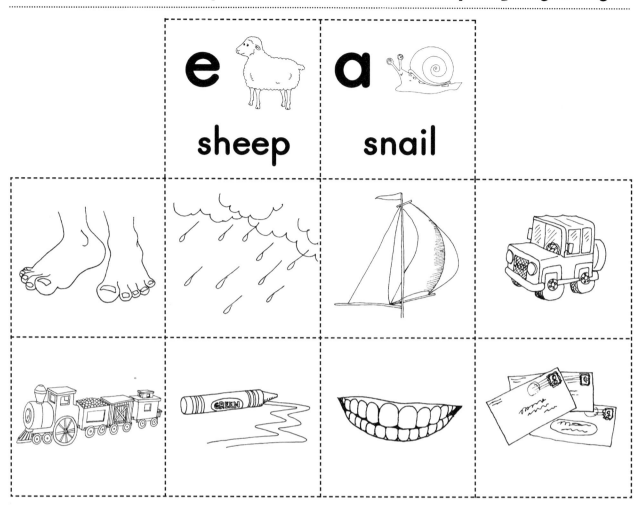

**#35** transitional level spellers  comparing long e/long a

| sleep | wheel | claim |
| --- | --- | --- |
| wait | meet | cheek |
| week | gain | queen |
| stain | braid | maid |
| | | |
| | | |
| | | |

#36 transitional level spellers    comparing long e/long a

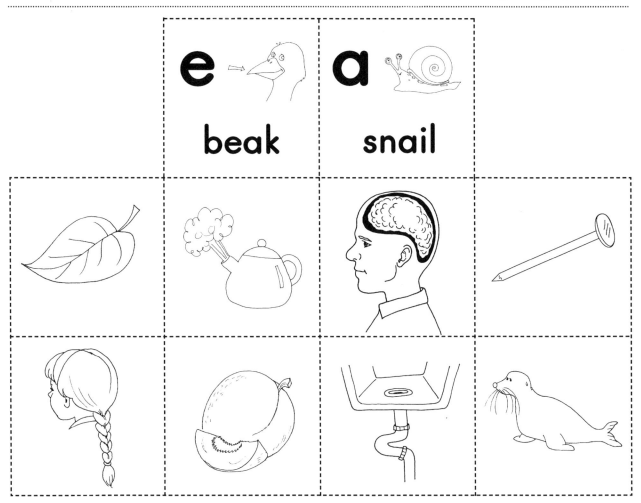

meal　pain

wait　peak

weak　gain

**#36** transitional level spellers — comparing long e/long a

| seam | clean | paint |
| mean | tail | rail |
| fail | seat | teach |
| beat | claim | grain |

# #37 transitional level spellers — comparing long e/long a

| chief | gait |
| wait | hair |
| grief | brief |

**#37** transitional level spellers　　　　comparing long e/long a

| fair | pair | shriek |
| rail | plain | field |
| bail | piece | shield |
| flair | priest | yield |

#38 transitional level spellers                    comparing long e/long o

#38 transitional level spellers — comparing long e/long o

| teeth | wheel | need |
|---|---|---|
| free | bleed | cheek |
| float | coach | coal |
| groan | roast | soak |

#39 transitional level spellers  comparing long e/long o

# #39 transitional level spellers — comparing long e/long o

| leash | groan | clean |
| --- | --- | --- |
| bead | foam | real |
| load | neat | road |
| seat | toast | boat |

# #40 transitional level spellers
## comparing long e/long o

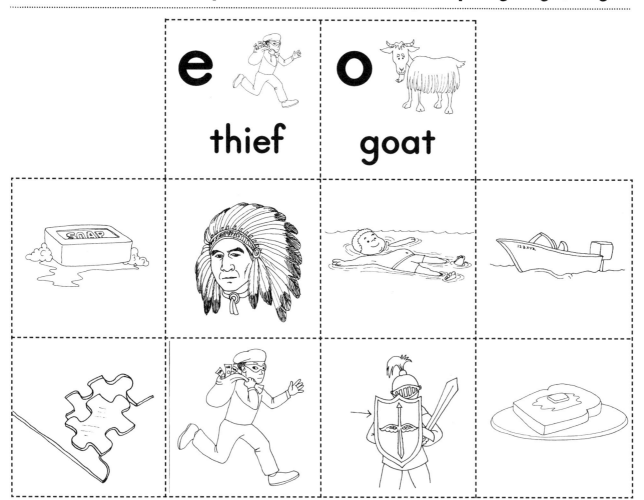

| grief | moan |
| road | field |
| thief | toad |

**#40** transitional level spellers — comparing long e/long o

| boast | soak | moat |
| --- | --- | --- |
| load | shriek | field |
| piece | belief | brief |
| priest | throat | whoa |
| | | |
| | | |
| | | |

#41 transitional level spellers — comparing long u/long a

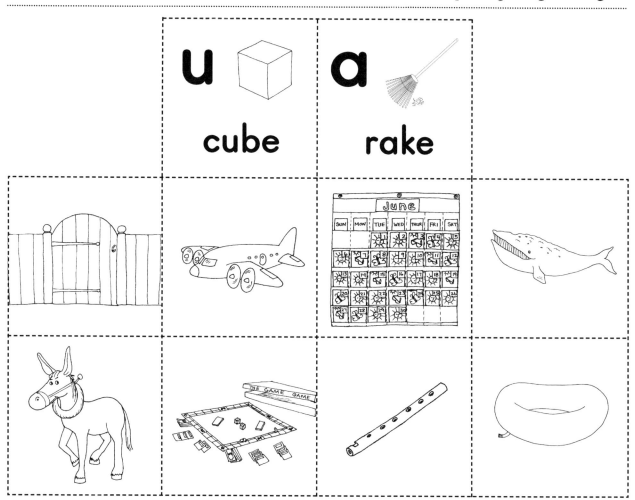

cute | rude
cage | base
huge | fake

**#41** transitional level spellers — comparing long u/long a

| prune | state | wave |
|---|---|---|
| fume | cape | rule |
| grape | dune | mane |
| tune | chute | jade |

# #42 transitional level spellers — comparing long u/long o

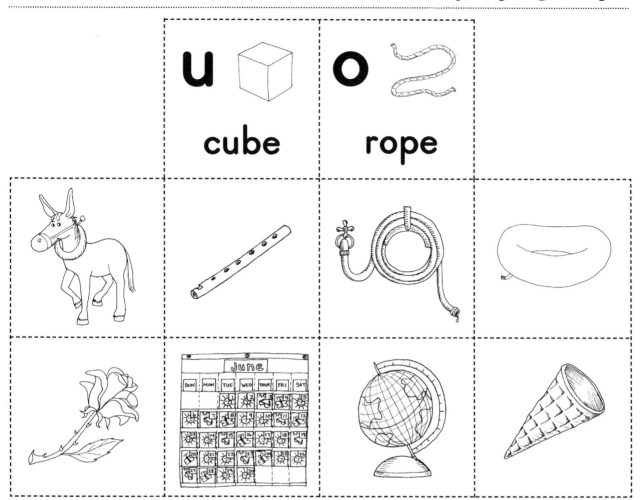

| tune | doze |
| mole | slap |
| rude | note |

**#42** transitional level spellers comparing long u/long o

| dune | joke | role |
| --- | --- | --- |
| cone | rule | phone |
| flute | mute | code |
| wrote | cute | prune |
| | | |
| | | |
| | | |

# #43 transitional level spellers     comparing long a/long o/long u

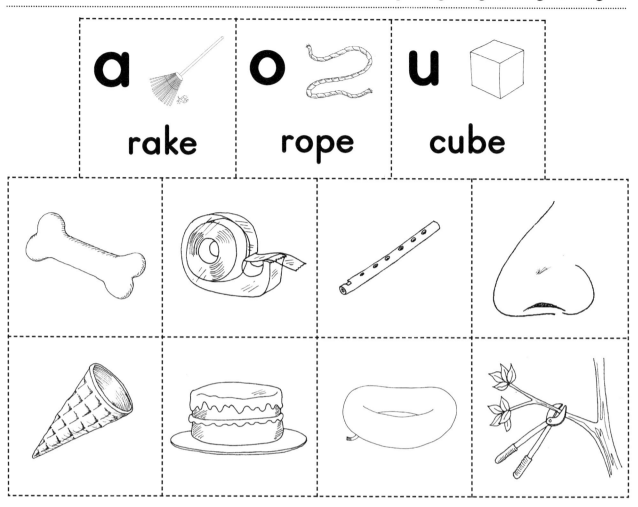

**#43** transitional level spellers     comparing long a/long o/long u

| stove | place | rule |
| --- | --- | --- |
| duke | shape | close |
| late | huge | sole |
| June | hope | sale |
|  |  |  |
|  |  |  |
|  |  |  |

#44 transitional level spellers　　comparing long u/long i

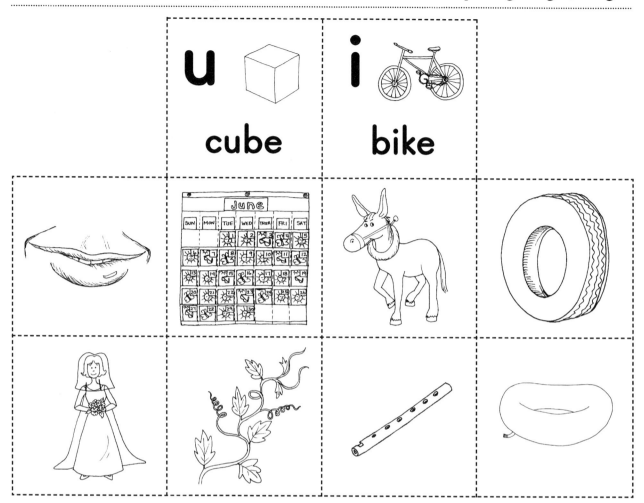

**#44** transitional level spellers — comparing long u/long i

| spice | fume | mute |
| --- | --- | --- |
| plume | site | lime |
| file | wipe | crude |
| rule | flute | write |

#45 transitional level spellers    comparing long a/long i/long u

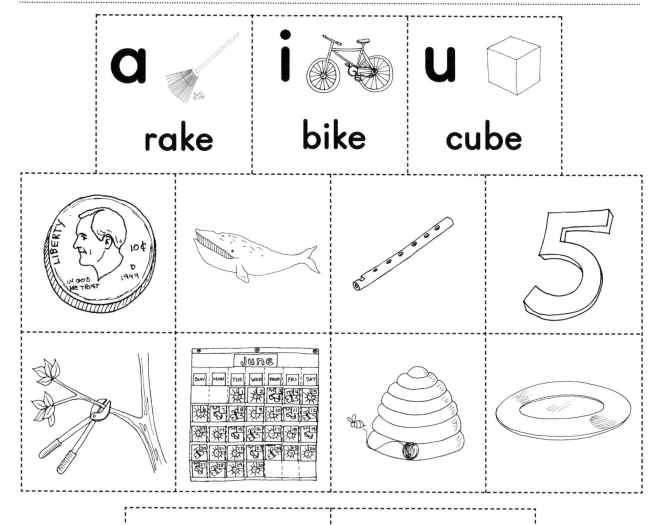

a — rake    i — bike    u — cube

cute    time

lace    tune

dive    safe

#45 transitional level spellers — comparing long a/long i/long u

| scale | prize | flute |
| --- | --- | --- |
| rude | rage | tale |
| space | rule | wife |
| ripe | slide | chute |

#46 transitional level spellers                comparing long u/long a

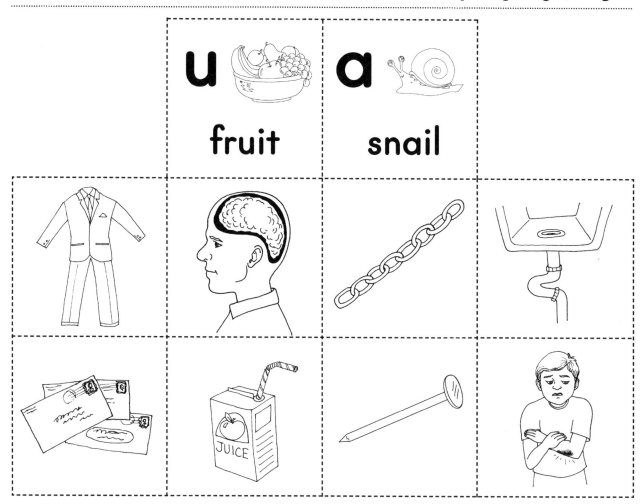

**#46** transitional level spellers — comparing long u/long a

| paint | fruit | sail |
|---|---|---|
| suit | bait | bruise |
| grain | faith | juice |
| cruise | quaint | claim |

#47 transitional level spellers    comparing long u/long o

**#47** transitional level spellers comparing long u/long o

| fruit | toast | croak |
| --- | --- | --- |
| moan | suit | load |
| roast | bruise | cloak |
| cruise | goal | juice |

# #48 transitional level spellers — comparing long a/long o/long u

**#48** transitional level spellers — comparing long a/long o/long u

| roam | load | stain |
| --- | --- | --- |
| cruise | sail | bruise |
| pain | suit | coach |
| fruit | toast | claim |

#49 transitional level spellers    comparing long u/long e

| suit | heel |
| beep | fruit |
| juice | meet |

# #49 transitional level spellers

comparing long u/long e

| cruise | speed | wheel |
| --- | --- | --- |
| beef | fruit | street |
| sweep | steel | bruise |
| suit | sneeze | juice |

#50 transitional level spellers    comparing long a/long e/long u

# #50 transitional level spellers — comparing long a/long e/long u

| meet | wait | suit |
| speech | juice | cruise |
| fruit | wheel | faith |
| stain | bruise | sheet |

#51 transitional level spellers  comparing long a/long e/long o

#51 transitional level spellers — comparing long a/long e/long o

| grow | play | grew |
|------|------|------|
| gray | know | chew |
| knew | show | way |
| stay | stew | blow |

# Appendix

## References

Bear, D., & Barone, D. (1998). *Developing Literacy: An Integrated Approach to Assessment and Instruction.* Boston: Houghton Mifflin Company.

Bear, D., Invernizzi, M., Templeton, S., & Johnston, F. (2003). *Words Their Way: Word Study for Phonics, Vocabulary, and Spelling Instruction, 3/E.* Upper Saddle River, NJ: Prentice Hall.

Invernizzi, M. (1992). The Vowel and What Follows: A Phonological Frame of Orthographic Analysis, pp. 105-136 in *Development of Orthographic Knowledge and the Foundations of Literacy: A Memorial Festschrift for Edmund H. Henderson.* Edited by S. Templeton & D. Bear Hillsdale, NJ: Lawrence Erlbaum.

Invernizzi, M., Abouzeid, M., & Gill, T. (1994). *Using Students' Invented Spelling As a Guide for Spelling Instruction That Emphasizes Word Study.* Elementary School Journal, (95(2), pp. 155-167).

Nielsen-Dunn, S. (2002). *Picture This!: Picture Sorting for Alphabetics, Phonemes, and Phonics.* San Diego, CA: Teaching Resource Center.

Pinnell, G., & Fountas, I. C., (1998). *Word Matters: Teaching Phonics and Spelling in the Reading/Writing Classroom.* Portsmouth, NH: Heinemann.

Vygotsky, L. S. (1978). *Mind in Society.* Cambridge, MA: Harvard University Press.

## Resources

**Available from Teaching Resource Center:**
*All Sorts of Sorts 1* by Sheron Brown (item #53520040)
*All Sorts of Sorts 2* by Sheron Brown (item #53520140)
Beginning Sound Card (item #53530350)
Beginning Sound Poster (item #53530370)
Beginning Sound Tent (item #53530360)
Beginning Blend/Digraph Sound Card (item #53530180)
Beginning Blend/Digraph Poster (item #53530190)
Beginning Sound Sort Cards (item #53530330)
*Literacy Task Cards, Set 1 (Word Building)* by Linda Dorn & Carla Soffos (item #53590290)
Long Vowel Pattern Sort Cards (item #53530260)
Magnetic Beginning Sound Picture Tiles (item #53500100)
*Picture This!* by Shari Nielson-Dunn (item#53520180)
Short Vowel Sort Cards (item #53530240)
*Words Thier Way, 3rd Edition* (item #62820150)
*Words Thier Way, Video* (item #62880010)

## Teaching Resource Center
**P. O. Box 82777, San Diego, CA 92138-2777**
**1-800-833-3389**
**www.trcabc.com**

# Index of Pictures

(horizontally by row from left to right)

## Section I: Short to Short

#1    mop, van, bat, fox  
hop, can, map, pot

#2    fan, hat, fin, gas  
pig, pan, pin, chin

#3    sun, rug, hug, bag  
van, jug, rat, bath

#4    hill, crib, crab, flag  
rat, brick, pin, map

#5    cob, kiss, hop, dish  
crib, hop, box, pig

#6    jump, gum, drill, dish  
pin, sun, fin, bug

#7    block, jam, fox, clock  
clap, doll, fan, bath

#8    peg, pot, stop, leg  
jet, ten, mop, cob

#9    frog, crib, cot, chick  
hop, pig, chin, doll

#10    doll, sun, cob, clock  
bug, hot, jug, rug

#11    fox, hen, men, hop  
chop, box, bed, bell

#12    run, neck, men, bug  
sun, ten, jug, dress

#13    skunk, plug, sun, bat  
pan, rat, rug, van

#14    bunk, mop, cob, block  
bug, gum, cub, doll

#15    thumb, chick, pin, truck  
hill, plug, jug, flipper

#16    dress, gum, bed, plug  
bunk, hen, bell, cub

## Section II: Short to Long

#17    fan, scale, tape, gas  
game, flag, ham, frame

#18    mail, map, sail, bag  
chain, can, hat, rain

#19    spray, play, crab, tray  
cash, bath, pay, map

#20    cone, mop, block, nose  
log, hose, frog, rose

#21    coat, road, doll, lock  
box, boat, cob, soap

#22    hop, blow, fox, clock  
throw, top, mow, bow

#23    five, vine, lip, dime  
pig, pin, dig, ride

#24    cry, kick, fry, mitt  
fly, pig, hit, sky

#25    night, hill, light, lid  
chick, tight, knit, bright

#26    jeep, hen, feet, teeth  
leg, deer, bed, bell

#27    beach, neck, men, beak  
jet, steam, leaf, dress

#28    skunk, tube, sun, hug  
flute, gum, june, prune

# Section III: Long to Long

#29  bone, hose, tape, cone
     game, skate, nose, frame

#30  mail, coat, sail, road
     chain, float, coach, rain

#31  spray, play, crow, tray
     bow, throw, pay, blow

#32  skate, hive, tape, bride
     frame, five, vine, game

#33  hose, vine, dime, robe
     hive, nose, cone, fire

#34  dice, store, plane, nine
     robe, kite, nose, game

#35  feet, rain, sail, jeep
     train, green, teeth, mail

#36  leaf, steam, brain, nail
     braid, peach, drain, seal

#37  chain, thief, drain, tail
     chief, paint, piece, shield

#38  queen, boat, feet, toast
     green, sleep, road, soap

#39  peach, coach, peas, boat
     road, steam, float, seal

#40  soap, chief, float, boat
     piece, thief, shield, toast

#41  gate, plane, june, whale
     mule, game, flute, tube

#42  mule, flute, hose, tube
     rose, june, globe, cone

#43  bone, tape, flute, nose
     cone, cake, tube, prune

#44  smile, june, mule, tire
     bride, vine, flute, tube

#45  dime, whale, flute, five
     prune, june, hive, plate

#46  suit, brain, chain, drain
     mail, juice, nail, bruise

#47  soap, juice, road, coach
     coat, float, suit, bruise

#48  braid, suit, drain, coat
     chain, soap, road, bruise

#49  queen, bruise, green, wheel
     juice, suit, feet, sneeze

#50  nail, juice, suit, bruise
     queen, green, brain, jeep

#51  bow, spray, throw, brew
     blow, tray, dew, pay

125

# Interested in Learning More About Word Study?

Author Shari Nielsen is available to develop custom workshops in Reading, Word Study, Spelling, Vocabulary and Meaning for your school site or district.

All the workshops focus on research based classroom practice. Workshops are presented in a hands-on learner-friendly format, designed to encourage effective practice in the classroom.

Each workshop begins with examining the current research around the topic to be presented, moving to assessing the students and determining where instruction should begin, and finally to the actual practice that would take place in the classroom setting. Management is heavily addressed through establishing routines and procedures around the topic being presented. Standards and test taking connections are always addressed.

To find out more about these exciting workshops call (775) 329-8449 or e-mail niel4@aol.com OR snielsen@washoe.k12.nv.us.